Hello, my name is Coco.

About me

My name is: ______________________

I am in Year: ______________________

Track your progress

As you complete pages in this book, trace over the matching letter here.

OXFORD UNIVERSITY PRESS

i
x
as in "box"
z
WELL DONE
b
h
c
o
a
d
q
g
u
y
TOP WORK

Before you begin writing …

Here are the 3Ps that will help you with your writing: posture, pencil grip and paper position. You will be reminded about these as you work through the book.

Posture

- Relax your arms.
- Sit back in your chair.
- Make sure your back is straight.

Put your feet flat on the floor.

Pencil grip

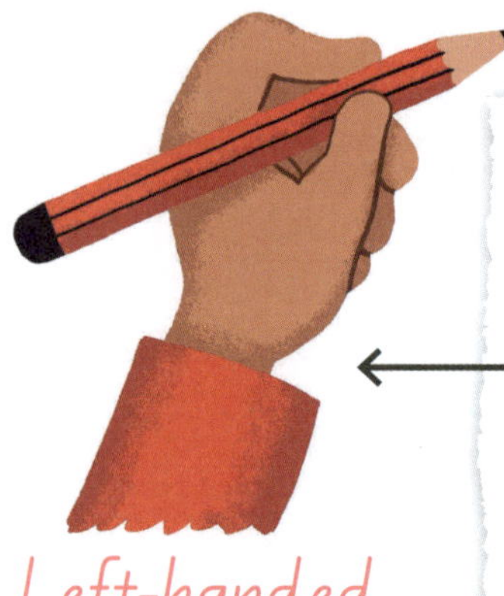

Left-handed

How you hold your pencil is important.

- Hold your pencil firmly between your thumb and index finger.
- Balance the pencil on your middle finger.
- Don't grip the pencil too tightly!

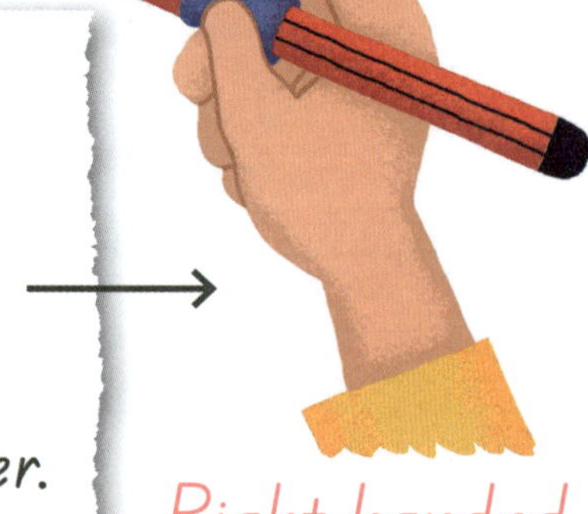

Right-handed

Paper position

Left-handed

- Tilt your page.
- Use your non-writing hand to steady the paper.

Right-handed

Hand and finger warm-ups

Crocodile snaps (whole arms)

Start with one arm straight above your head and the other extended down one side of your body. Snap your hands together, like a crocodile snapping its jaws. Repeat, with your other arm above your head.

Open, shut them (hands)

Open, shut them. Open, shut them.
Give a little clap.
Open, shut them. Open, shut them.
Lay them in your lap.
Repeat.

Spider push-ups (fingers)

Place your fingertips together. Bend and straighten your fingers while pushing your fingertips against each other.

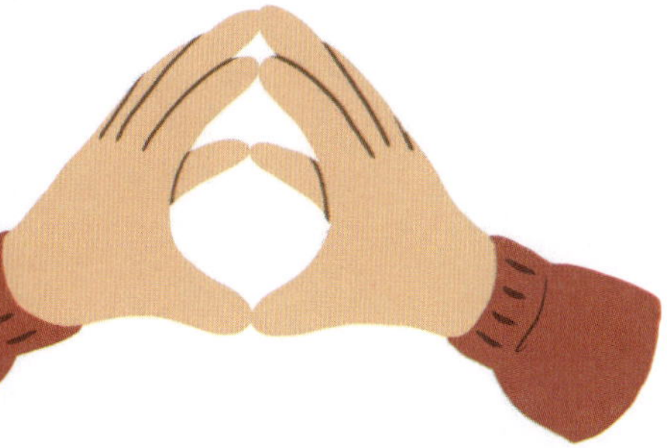

Warm-up patterns

Trace the grey lines.

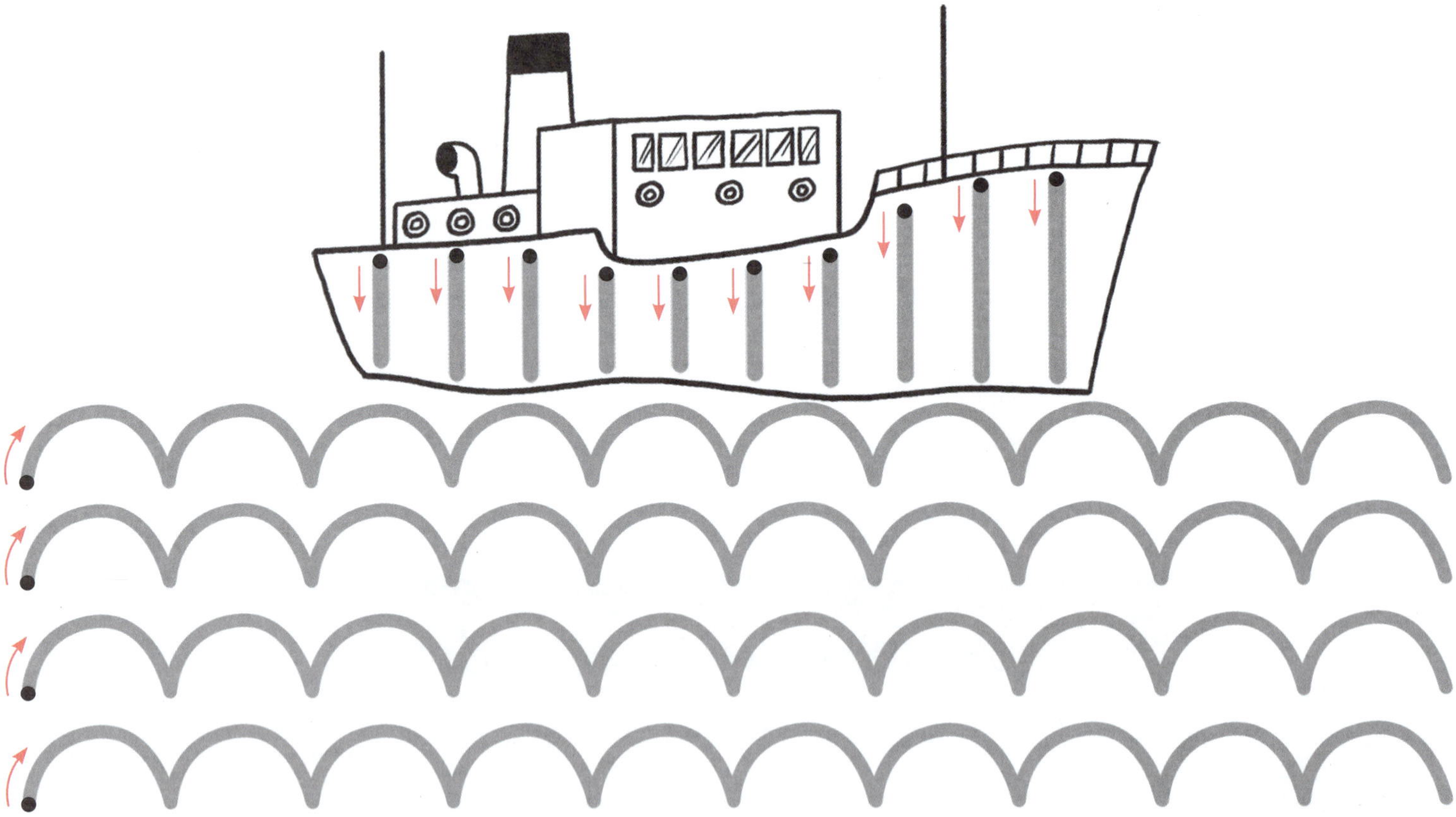

Trace the grey lines.

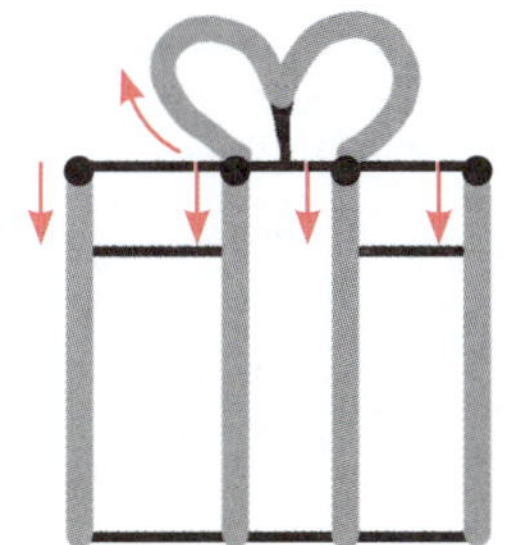

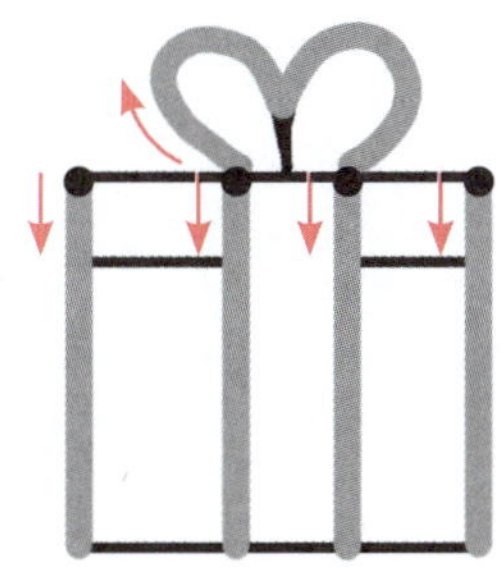

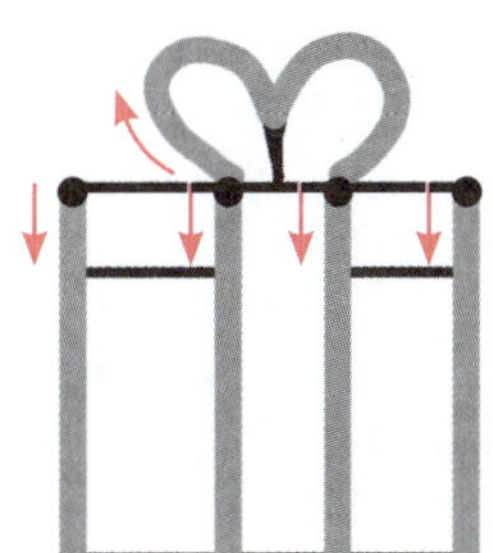

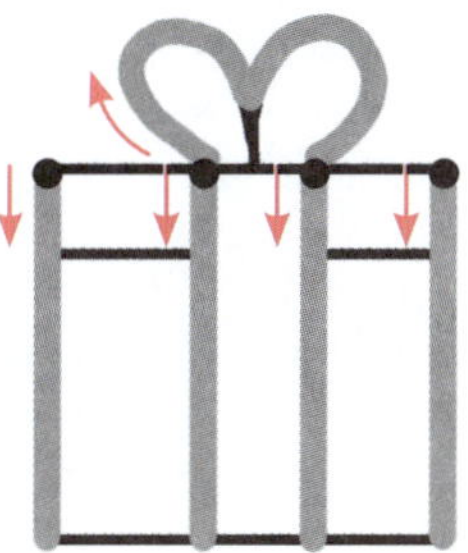

Have you checked your posture, pencil grip and paper position?

Have you done your warm-ups?

list

Track, trace and copy the letters and words.

let lid legs lap letter

let

ladder less list loop left

ladder

Trace.

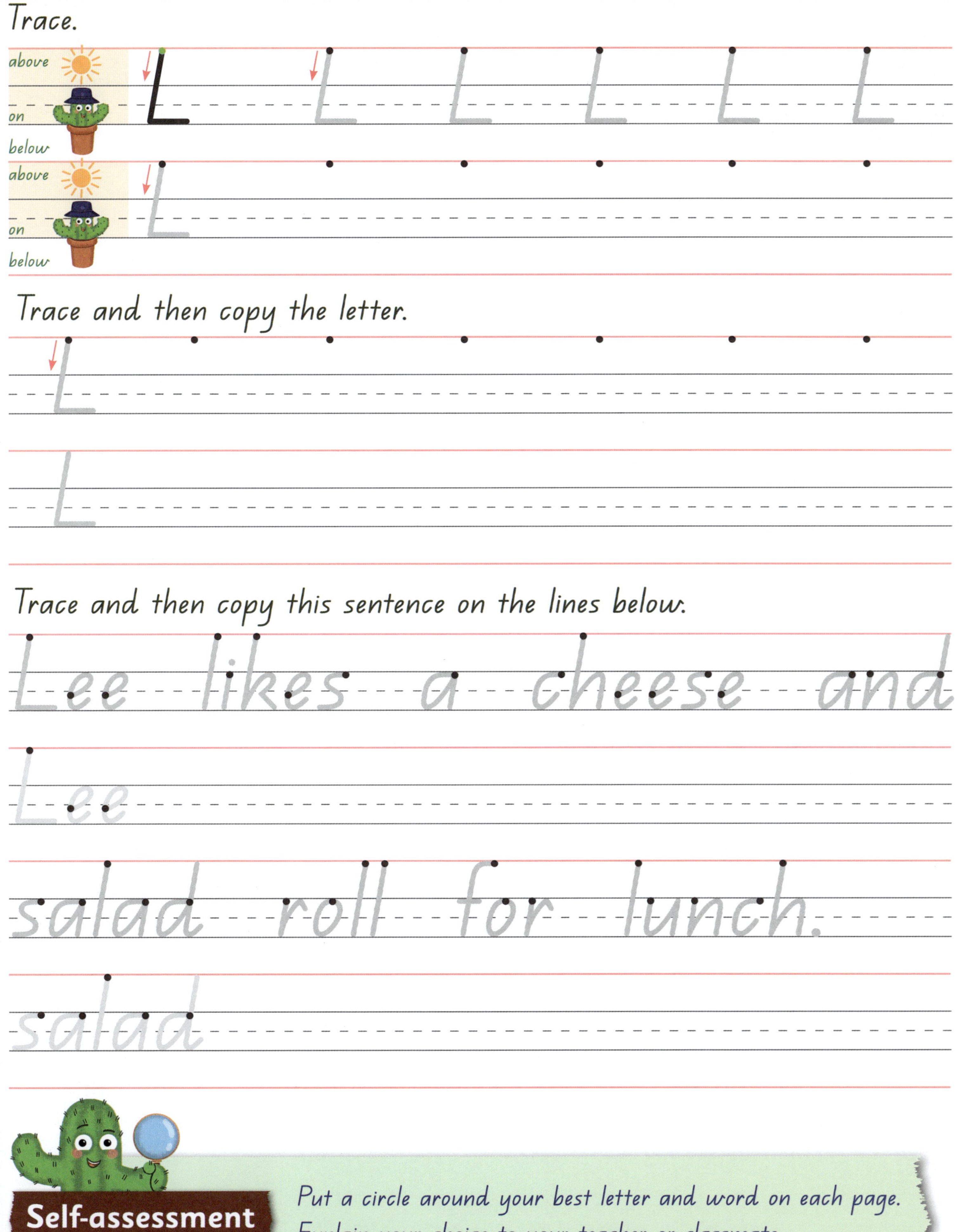

Trace and then copy the letter.

Trace and then copy this sentence on the lines below.

Self-assessment

Put a circle around your best letter and word on each page.
Explain your choice to your teacher or classmate.

Have you checked your posture, pencil grip and paper position?

Have you done your warm-ups?

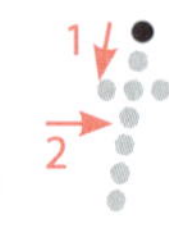
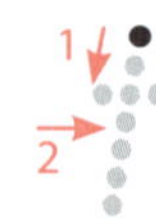
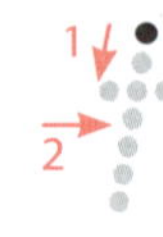

train

Track, trace and copy the letters and words.

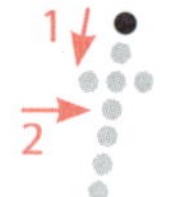

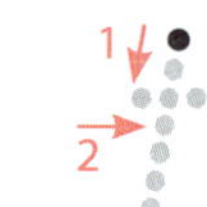

1 2 t t t t t t t

t

this them then that

this

tag tall tail tank tap

tag

OXFORD UNIVERSITY PRESS

Trace.

Trace and then copy the letter.

Trace and then copy this sentence on the lines below.

Tess and Tim went into

town on the train.

Self-assessment

Put a circle around your best letter and word on each page. Explain your choice to your teacher or classmate.

Have you checked your posture, pencil grip and paper position?

Have you done your warm-ups?

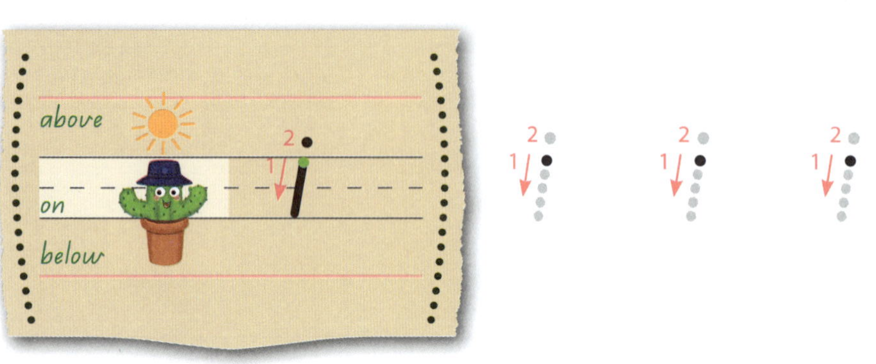

inside

Track, trace and copy the letters and words.

i i i i i i i

i

if it in is inside into

if

ill ink insect item index

ill

OXFORD UNIVERSITY PRESS

Trace.

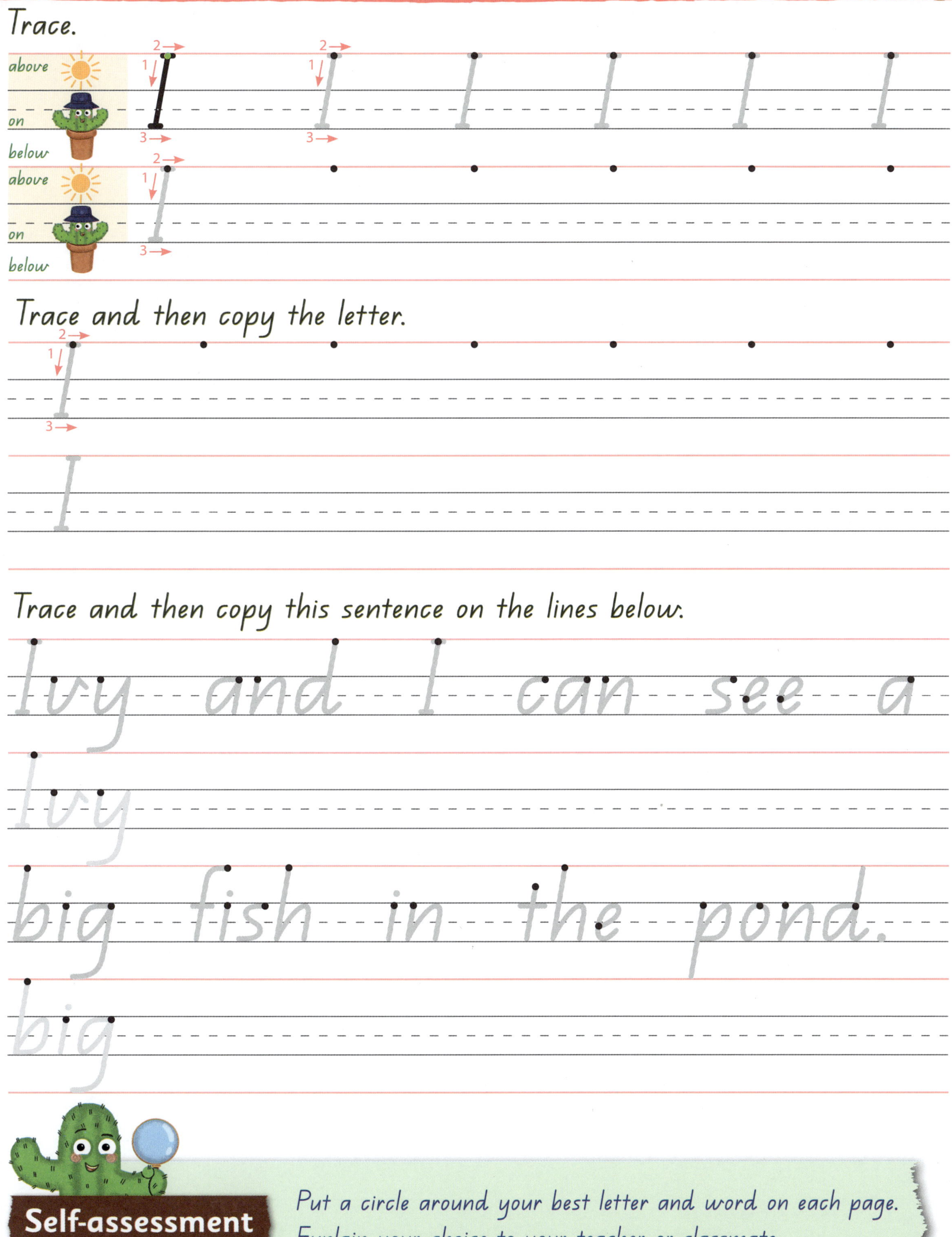

Trace and then copy the letter.

Trace and then copy this sentence on the lines below.

Self-assessment

Put a circle around your best letter and word on each page. Explain your choice to your teacher or classmate.

Have you checked your posture, pencil grip and paper position?

Have you done your warm-ups?

Track, trace and copy the letters and words.

x as in "box"

x x x x x x x

x

box six mix wax text

box

relax taxi fox exit

relax

Trace.

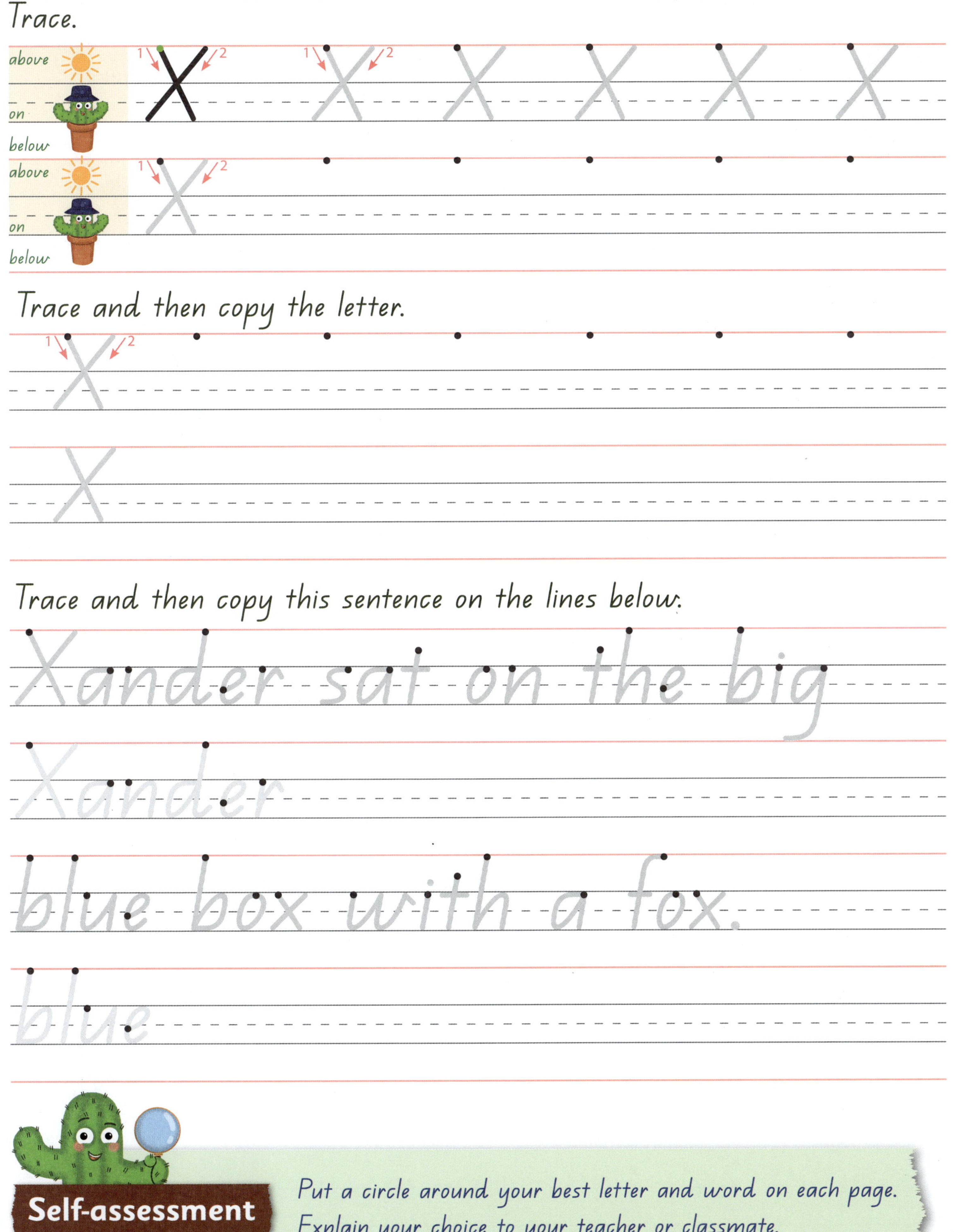

Trace and then copy the letter.

Trace and then copy this sentence on the lines below.

Self-assessment

Put a circle around your best letter and word on each page. Explain your choice to your teacher or classmate.

Have you checked your posture, pencil grip and paper position?

Have you done your warm-ups?

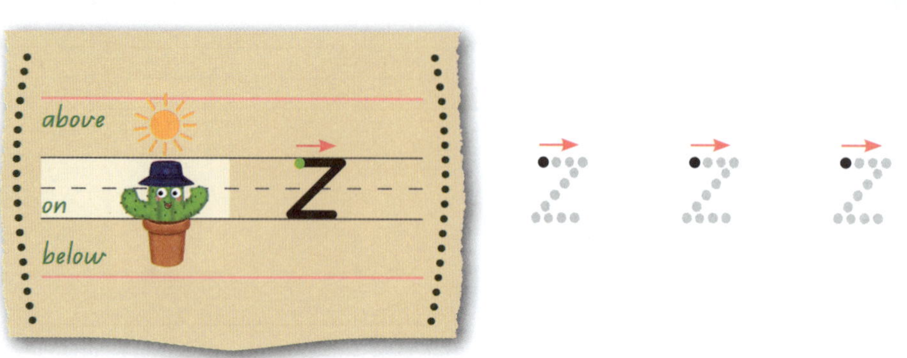

z z z

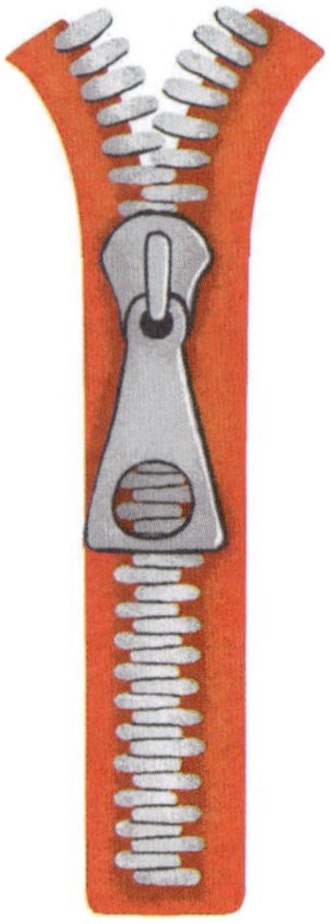

Track, trace and copy the letters and words.

z z z z z z z

zip

z z z z z z z

z

zig zag zap zip

zig

zoo zoom haze maze

zoo

Trace.

Trace and then copy the letter.

Trace and then copy this sentence on the lines below.

Self-assessment

Put a circle around your best letter and word on each page. Explain your choice to your teacher or classmate.

Have you checked your posture, pencil grip and paper position?

Have you done your warm-ups?

above
on
below

h h h

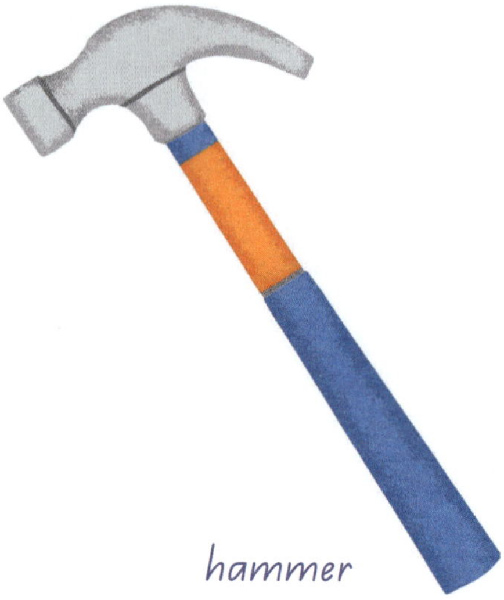

hammer

Track, trace and copy the letters and words.

h h h h h h h

h h h h h h h

h

had hot his hammer

had

hair hard hiss heel

hair

Trace.

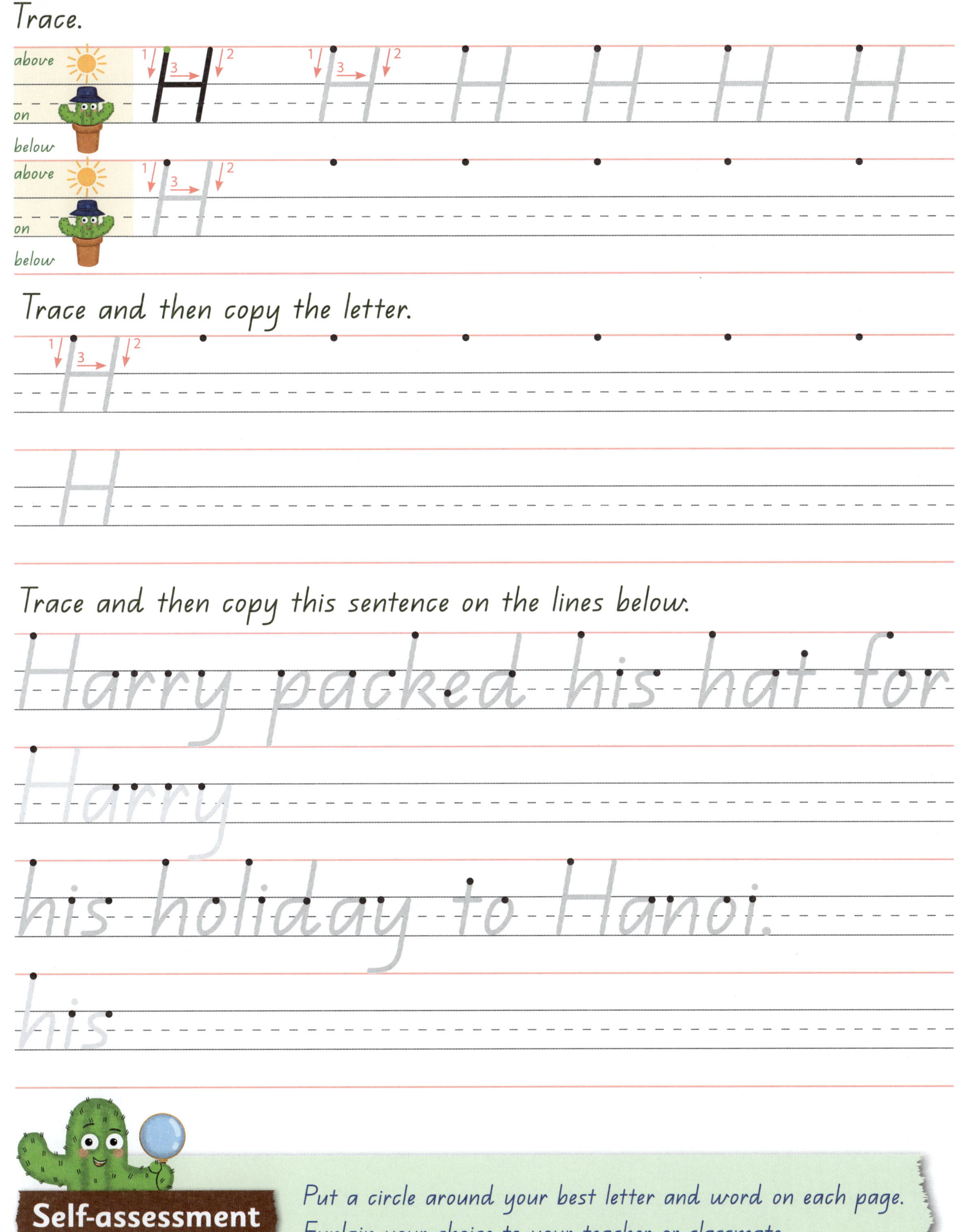

Trace and then copy the letter.

Trace and then copy this sentence on the lines below.

Self-assessment

Put a circle around your best letter and word on each page.
Explain your choice to your teacher or classmate.

Have you checked your posture, pencil grip and paper position?

Have you done your warm-ups?

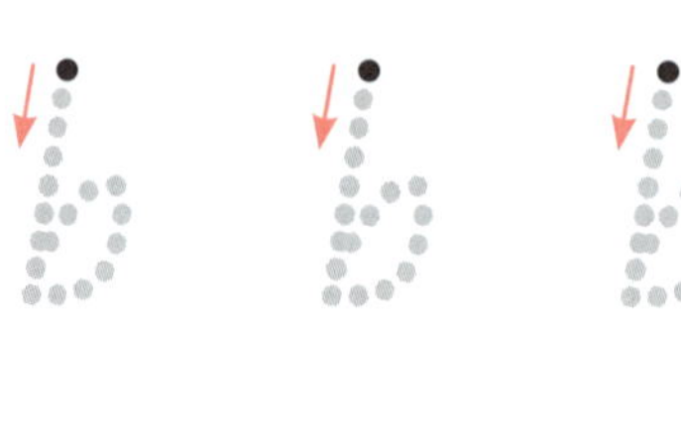

bed

Track, trace and copy the letters and words.

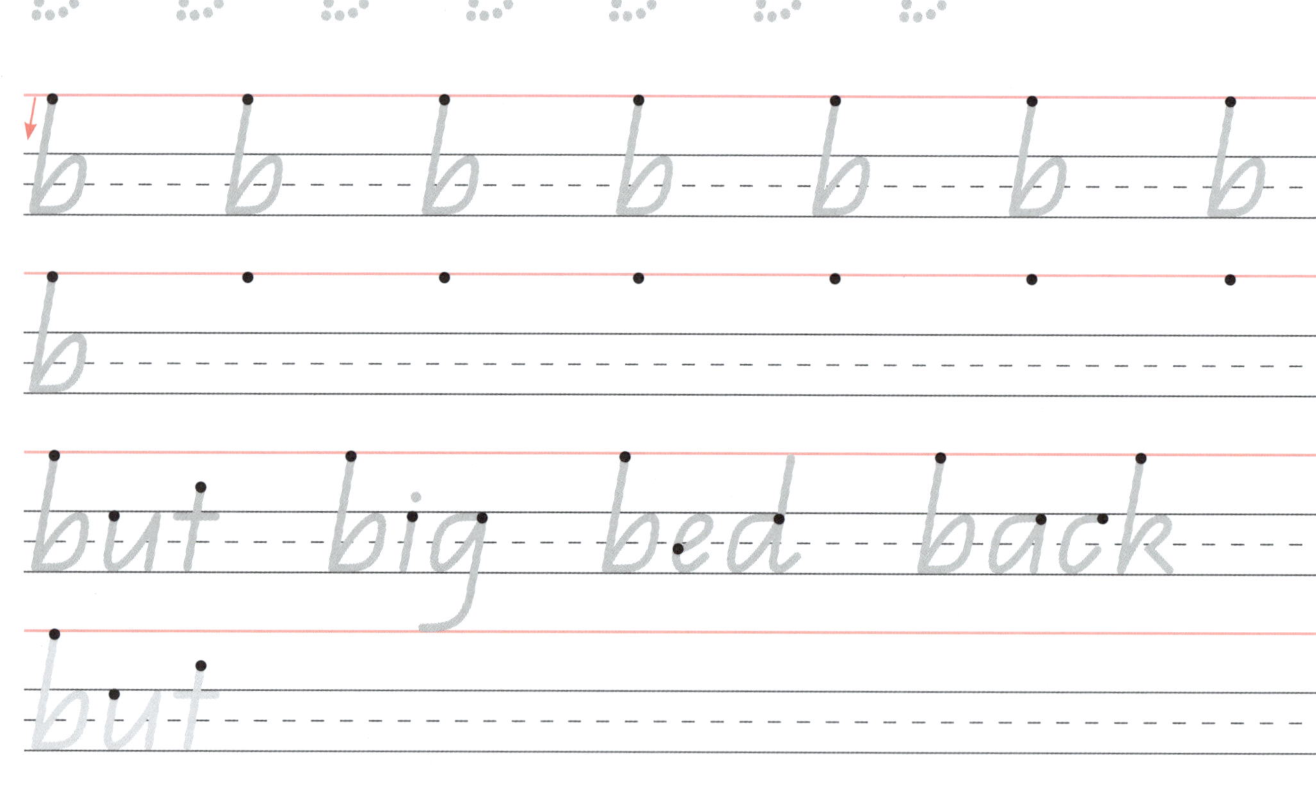

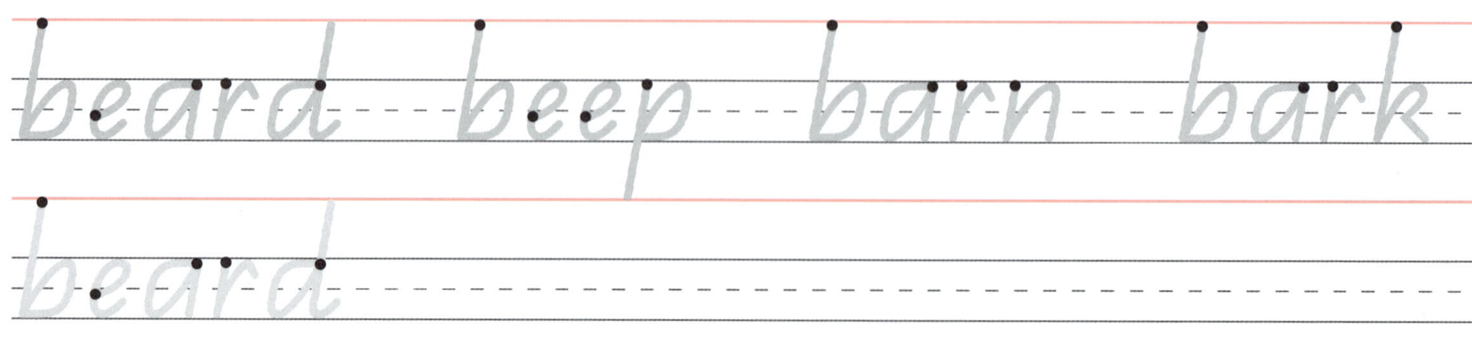

Trace.

Self-assessment

Put a circle around your best letter and word on each page.
Explain your choice to your teacher or classmate.

Have you checked your posture, pencil grip and paper position?

Have you done your warm-ups?

k k k

key

Track, trace and copy the letters and words.

k k k k k k k

k k k k k k k

k

kit king kittens keen

kit

keep kids kiss kick key

keep

OXFORD UNIVERSITY PRESS

Trace.

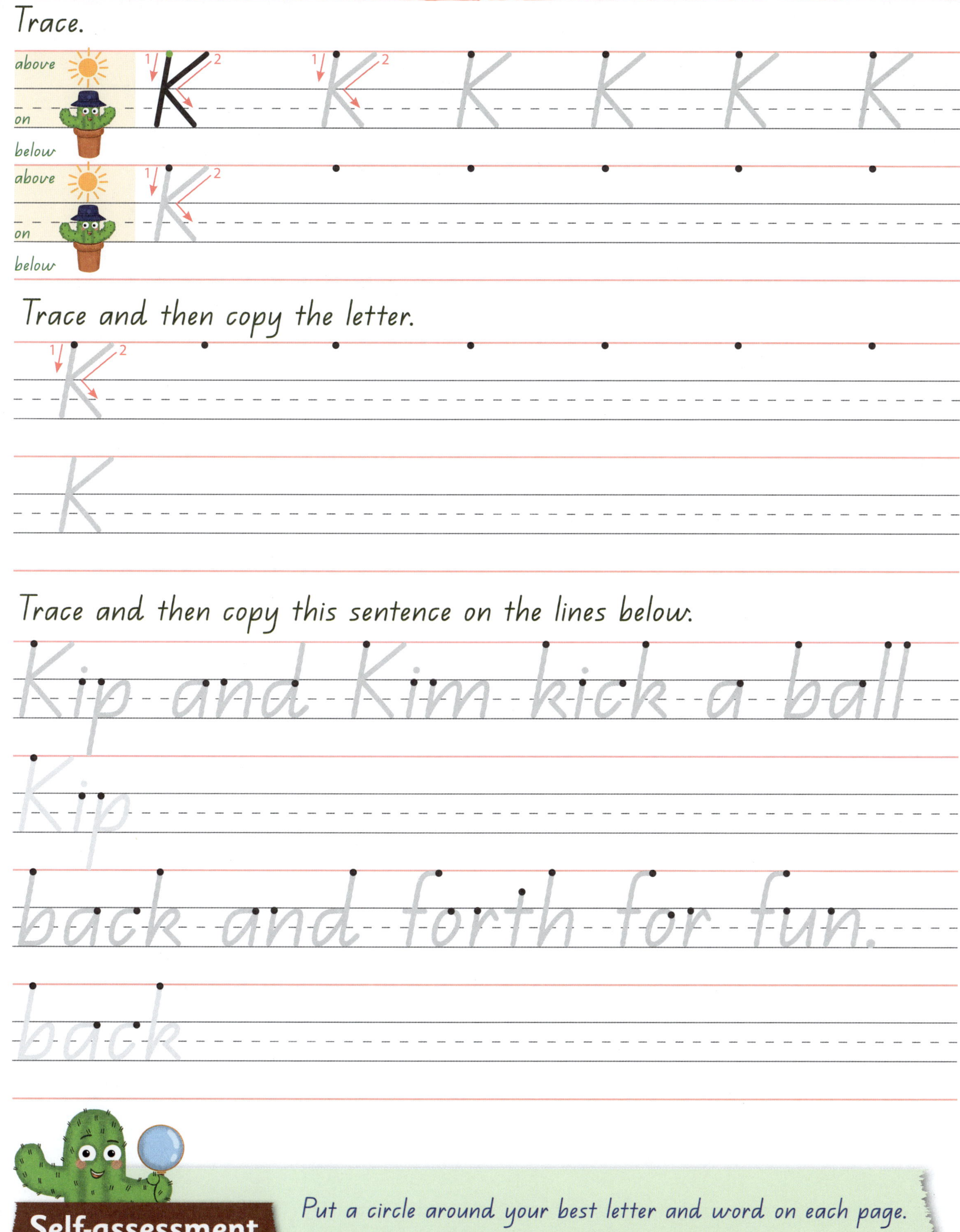

Trace and then copy the letter.

Trace and then copy this sentence on the lines below.

Self-assessment

Put a circle around your best letter and word on each page.
Explain your choice to your teacher or classmate.

Have you checked your posture, pencil grip and paper position?

Have you done your warm-ups?

rug

Track, trace and copy the letters and words.

r r r r r r r

r r r r r r r

r

ran run red rap rag

ran

rain rug rocket rat

rain

Trace.

Trace and then copy the letter.

Trace and then copy this sentence on the lines below.

Self-assessment

Put a circle around your best letter and word on each page. Explain your choice to your teacher or classmate.

Have you checked your posture, pencil grip and paper position?

Have you done your warm-ups?

n n n

note

Track, trace and copy the letters and words.

n n n n n n n

n n n n n n n

n

note next no near nail

note

nod north now not nut

nod

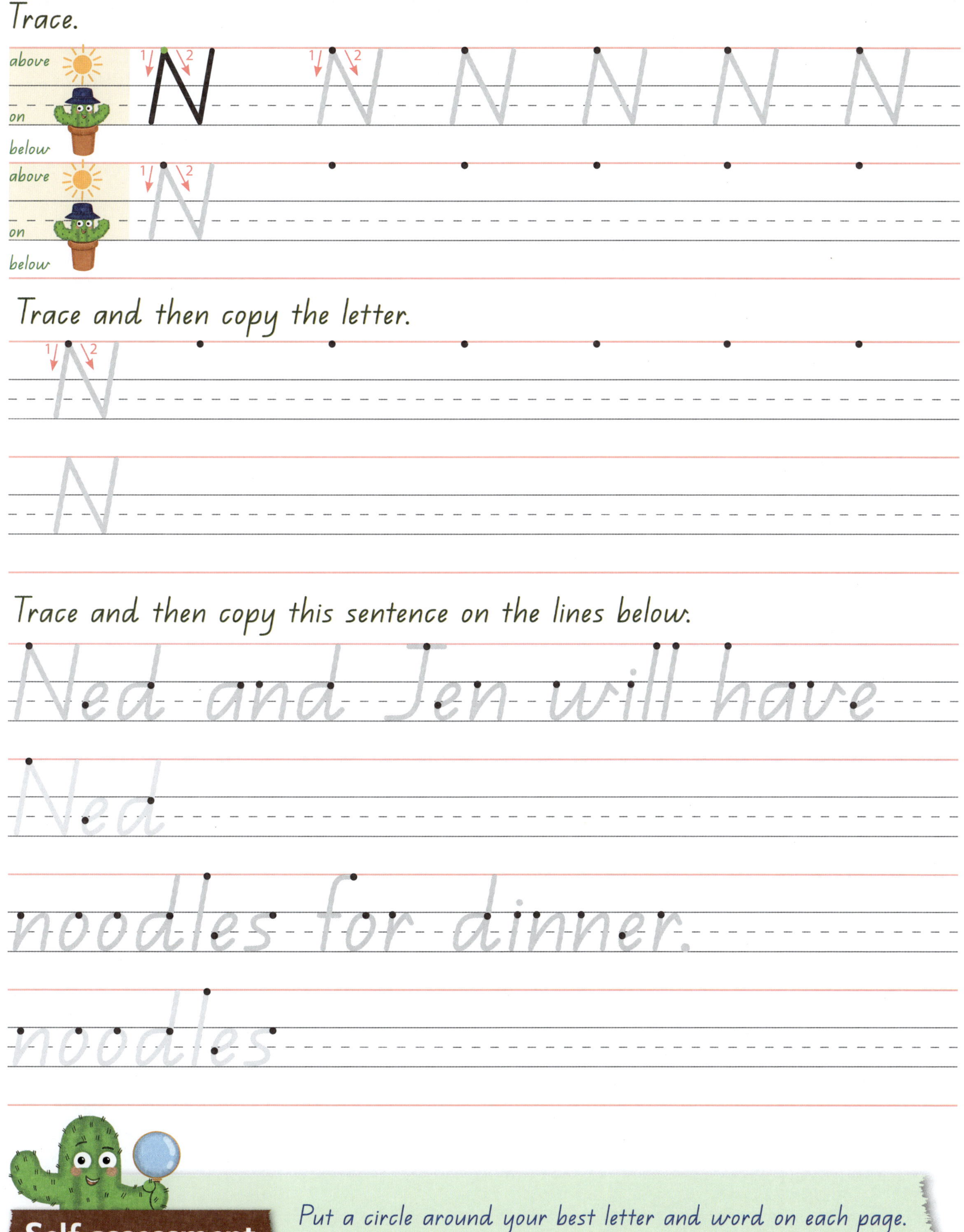

Self-assessment

Put a circle around your best letter and word on each page.
Explain your choice to your teacher or classmate.

Have you checked your posture, pencil grip and paper position?

Have you done your warm-ups?

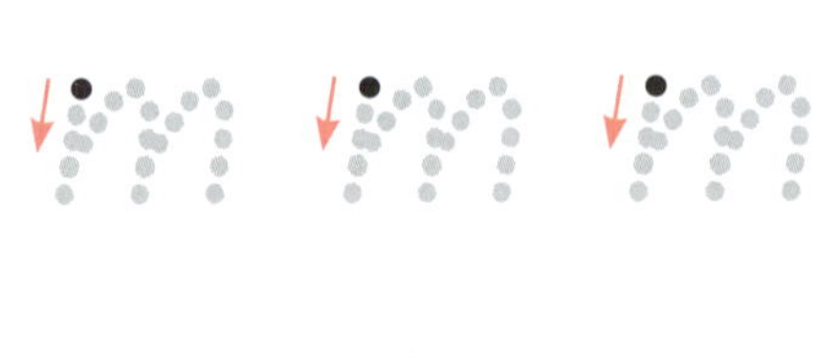

mess

Track, trace and copy the letters and words.

m m m m m m m

m m m m m m m

m

man moon mess mum

man

mail maid march mud

mail

Trace.

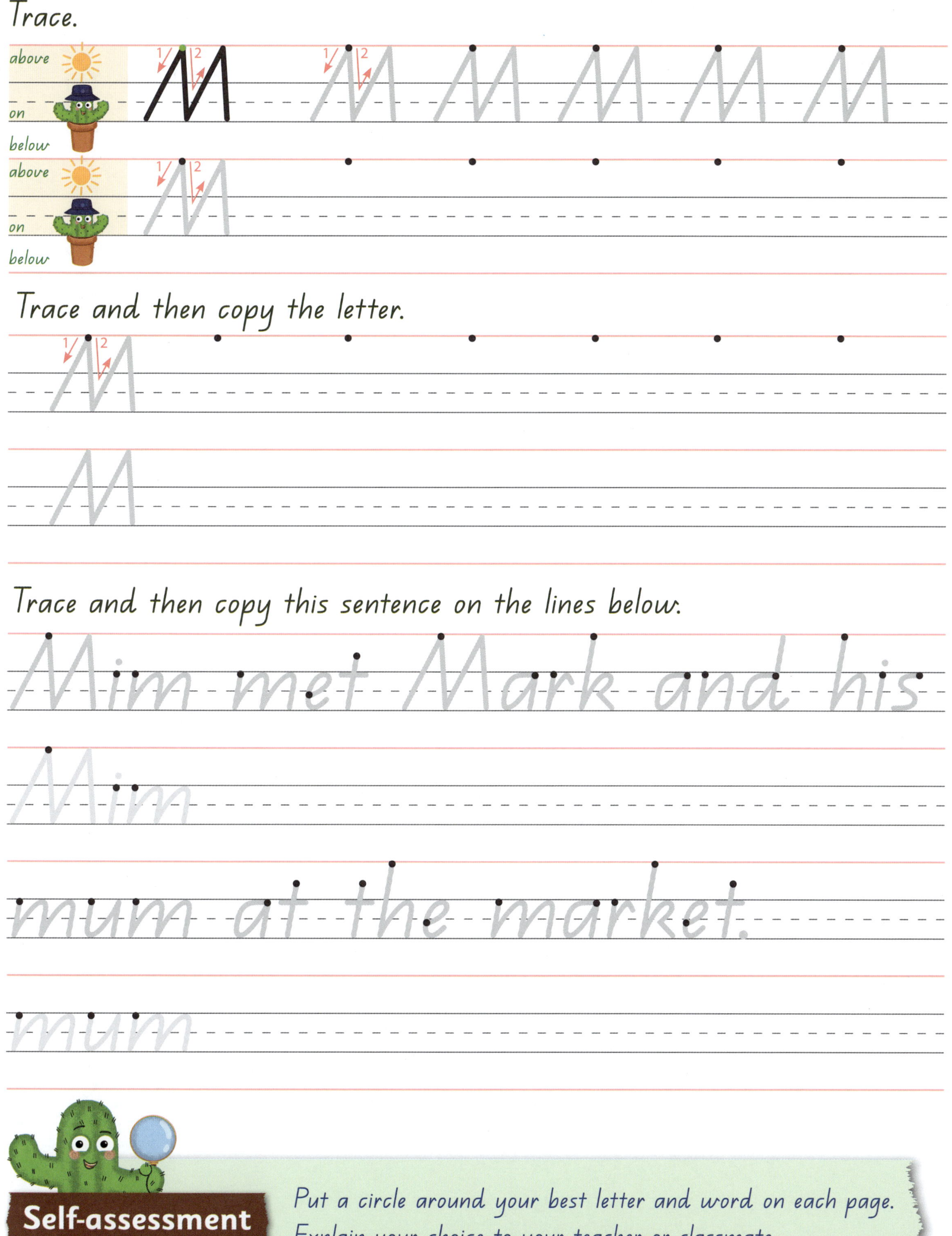

Trace and then copy the letter.

Trace and then copy this sentence on the lines below.

Mim met Mark and his mum at the market.

Self-assessment

Put a circle around your best letter and word on each page. Explain your choice to your teacher or classmate.

Have you checked your posture, pencil grip and paper position?

Have you done your warm-ups?

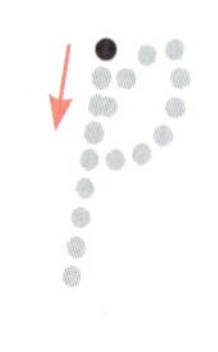

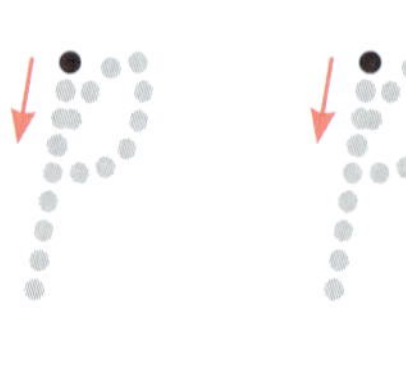

plant

Track, trace and copy the letters and words.

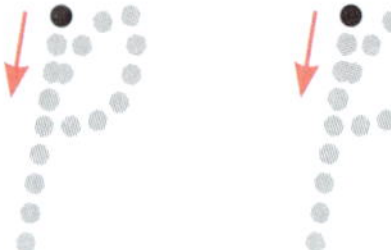

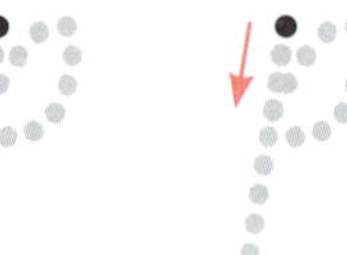

p p p p p p p

p

pink pack plants puff

pink

porch power port pip

porch

Trace.

Trace and then copy the letter.

Trace and then copy this sentence on the lines below.

Self-assessment

Put a circle around your best letter and word on each page. Explain your choice to your teacher or classmate.

Have you checked your posture, pencil grip and paper position?

Have you done your warm-ups?

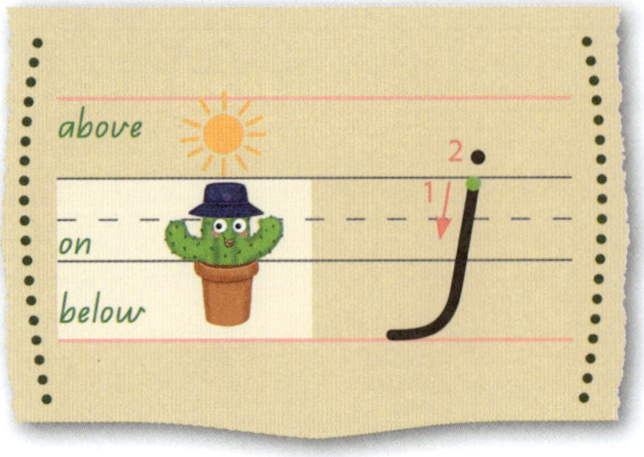

above

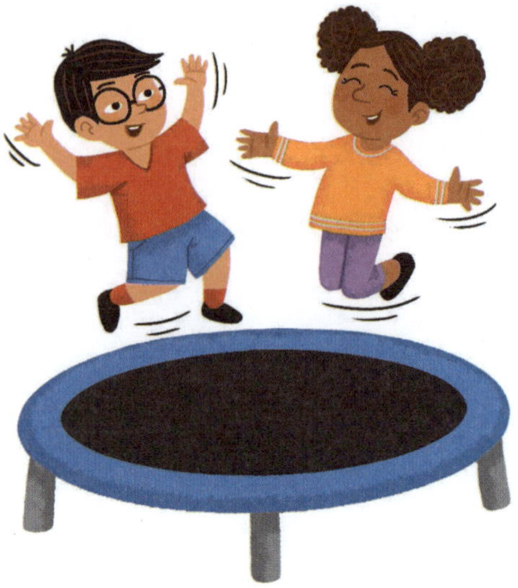

on

below

Track, trace and copy the letters and words.

jump

jog job jets just joy

jog

jacket jam join jump

jacket

Trace.

Trace and then copy the letter.

Trace and then copy this sentence on the lines below.

Jez and Jo jump with joy over the jam jars.

Self-assessment

Put a circle around your best letter and word on each page. Explain your choice to your teacher or classmate.

Warm-up patterns

Trace the grey lines.

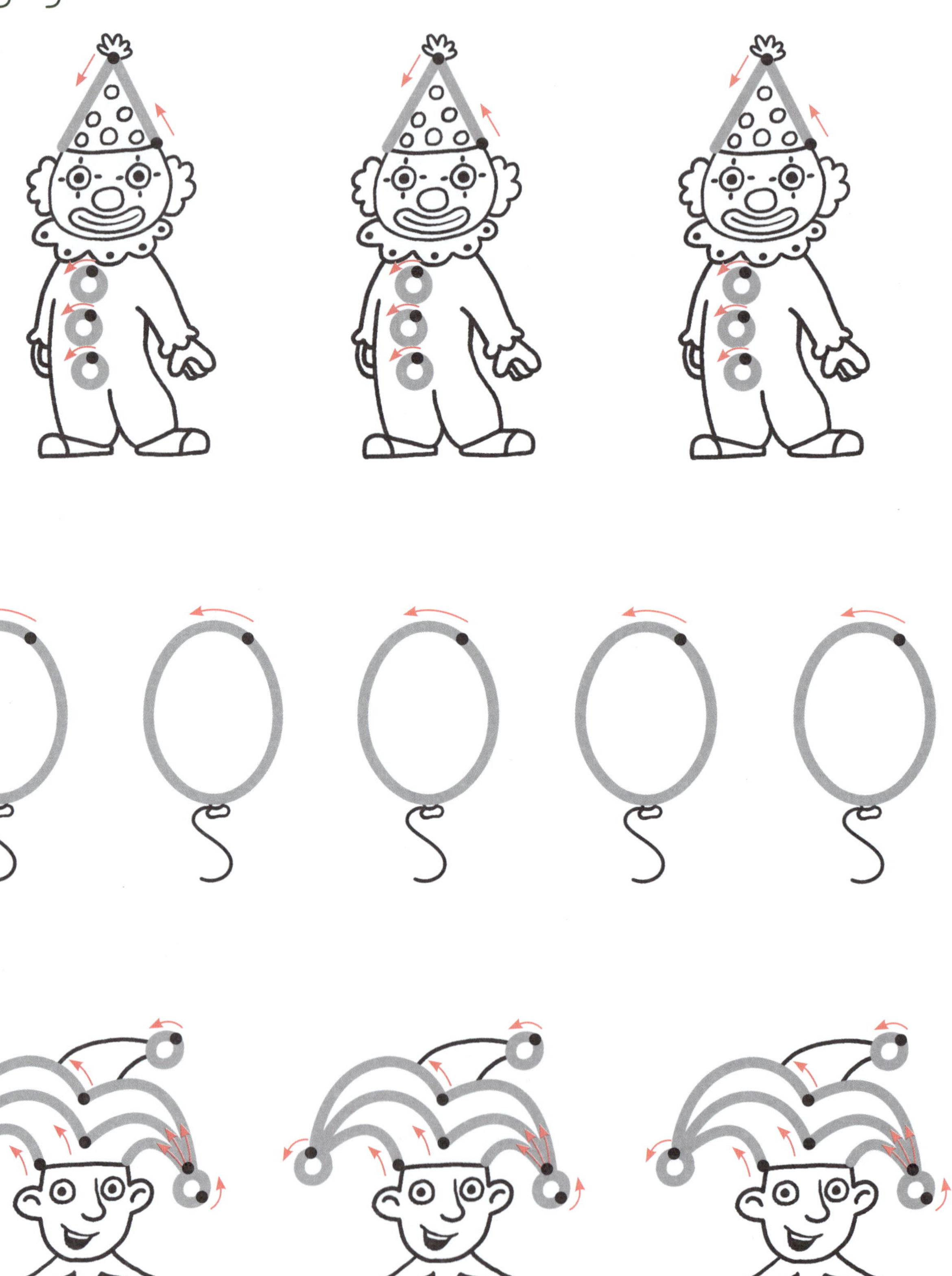

OXFORD UNIVERSITY PRESS

Trace the grey lines.

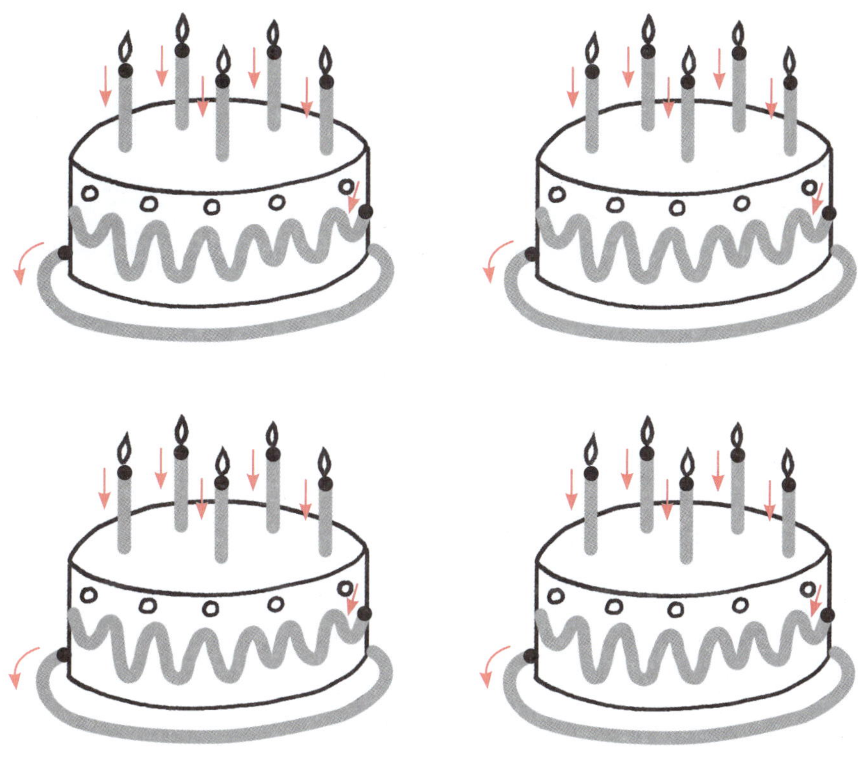

Have you checked your posture, pencil grip and paper position?

Have you done your warm-ups?

clouds

Track, trace and copy the letters and words.

c c c c c c c

can cool cat chair cloud

can

chess chick chatter curl

chess

Trace.

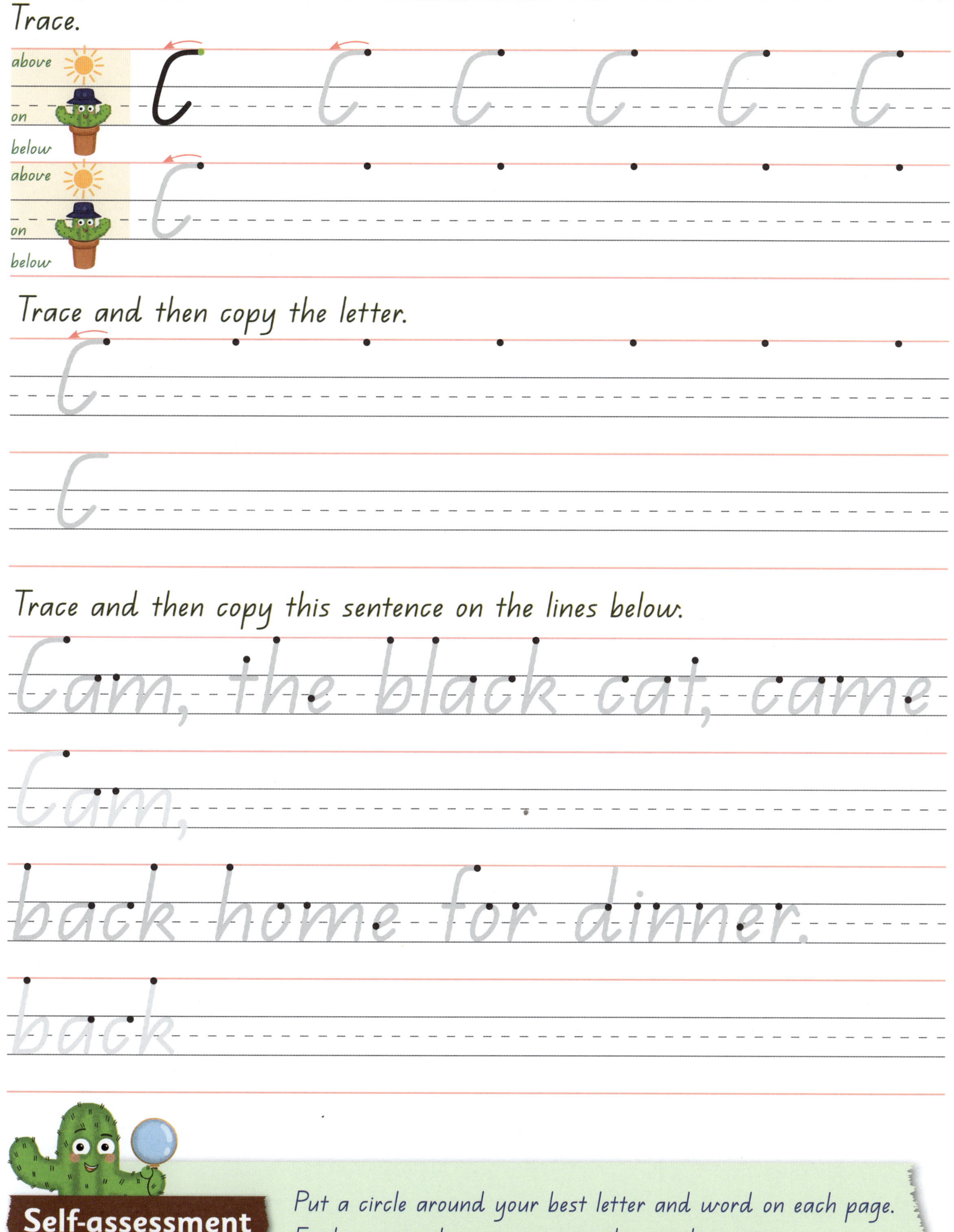

Trace and then copy the letter.

Trace and then copy this sentence on the lines below.

Cam, the black cat, came

back home for dinner.

Self-assessment

Put a circle around your best letter and word on each page. Explain your choice to your teacher or classmate.

3Ps Have you checked your posture, pencil grip and paper position?

Have you done your warm-ups?

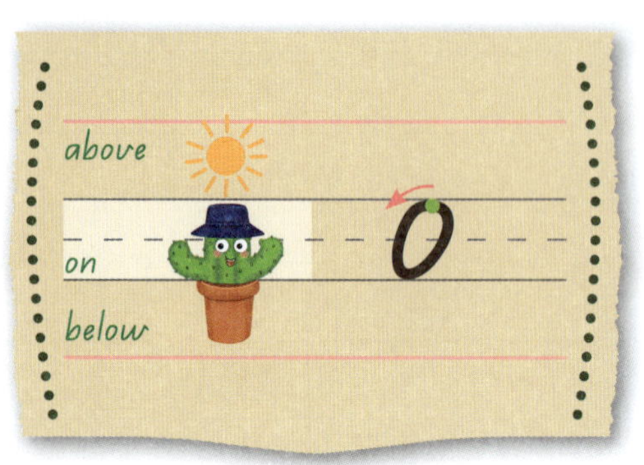

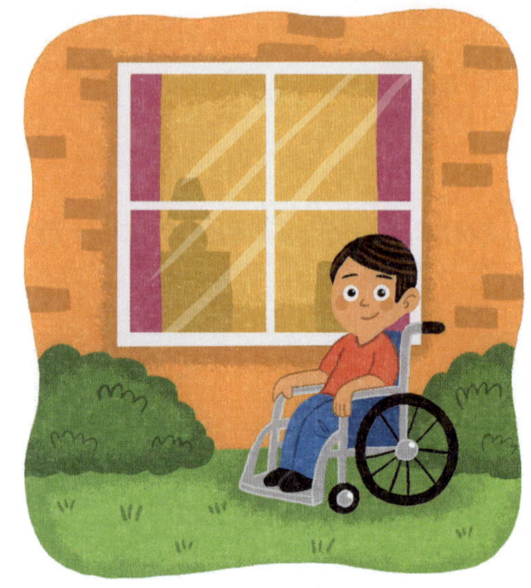

o o o

Track, trace and copy the letters and words.

outside

o o o o o o o

o o o o o o o

o

on off outside odd

on

oats oil order owl old

oats

Trace.

Self-assessment

Put a circle around your best letter and word on each page. Explain your choice to your teacher or classmate.

Have you checked your posture, pencil grip and paper position?

Have you done your warm-ups?

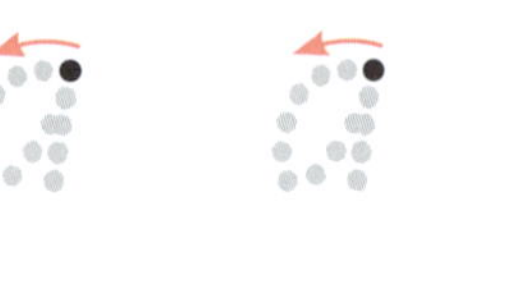

ant

Track, trace and copy the letters and words.

a a a a a a a

a a a a a a a

a

an am and as ant

an

airport arch arm ash

airport

Trace.

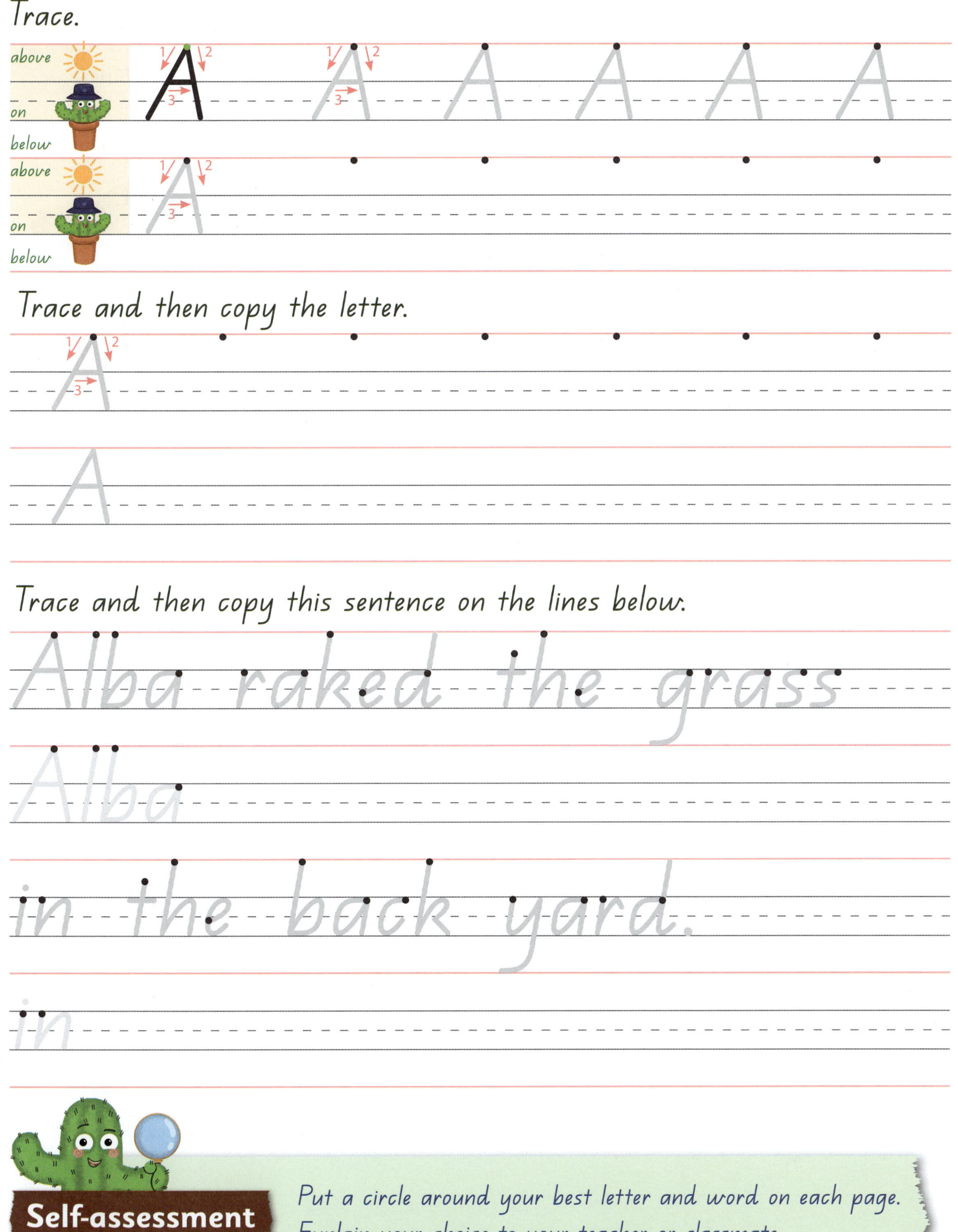

Trace and then copy the letter.

Trace and then copy this sentence on the lines below.

Self-assessment

Put a circle around your best letter and word on each page. Explain your choice to your teacher or classmate.

Have you checked your posture, pencil grip and paper position?

Have you done your warm-ups?

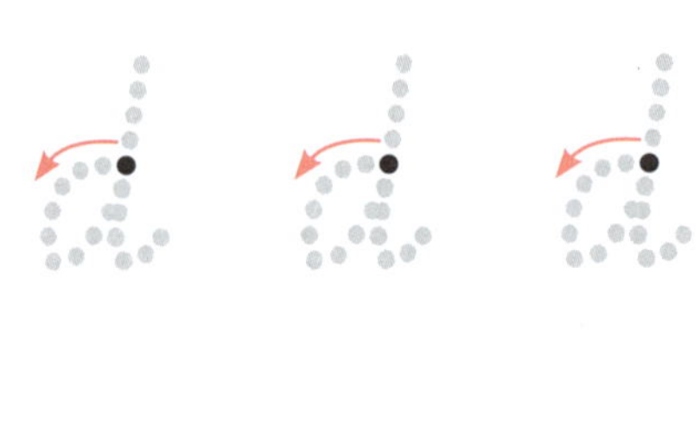

Track, trace and copy the letters and words.

d d d d d d d

doll

d d d d d d d

d

did dog doll do dot

did

dash deck dear dark

dash

Trace.

Self-assessment

Put a circle around your best letter and word on each page.
Explain your choice to your teacher or classmate.

Have you checked your posture, pencil grip and paper position?

Have you done your warm-ups?

g g g

grandma

Track, trace and copy the letters and words.

g g g g g g g

g g g g g g g

g

got going get grandma

got

gather good gum gear

gather

Trace.

Trace and then copy the letter.

Trace and then copy this sentence on the lines below.

Gus got a good big long hug from Gran.

Self-assessment

Put a circle around your best letter and word on each page. Explain your choice to your teacher or classmate.

Have you checked your posture, pencil grip and paper position?

Have you done your warm-ups?

q q q

quack

Track, trace and copy the letters and words.

q q q q q q q

q q q q q q q

q

quiz quack quick quit

quiz

queen quiver quip

queen

Trace.

above

on

below

Q Q Q Q Q Q

above

on

below

Q

Trace and then copy the letter.

Q

Q

Trace and then copy this sentence on the lines below.

Quin the duck quacks

Quin

near the little pond.

near

Self-assessment

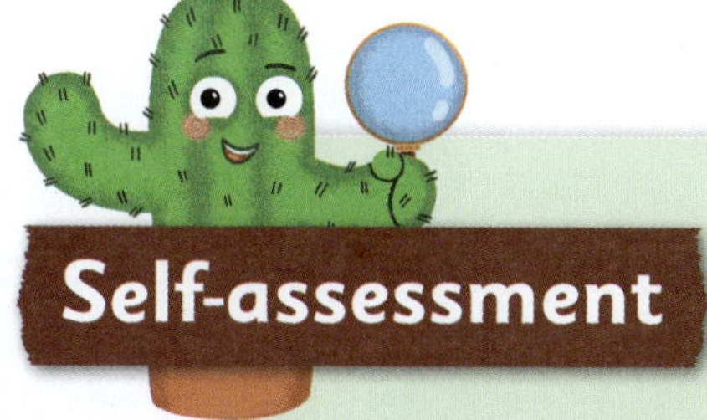

Put a circle around your best letter and word on each page.
Explain your choice to your teacher or classmate.

Have you checked your posture, pencil grip and paper position?

Have you done your warm-ups?

egg

Track, trace and copy the letters and words.

e e e e e e e

e

egg eat each evening eel

egg

ever exit escape enjoy

ever

Trace.

above
on
below

E E E E E E

above
on
below

E

Trace and then copy the letter.

E

E

Trace and then copy this sentence on the lines below.

Each day for lunch, Eva

Each

eats an egg with cheese.

eats

Self-assessment

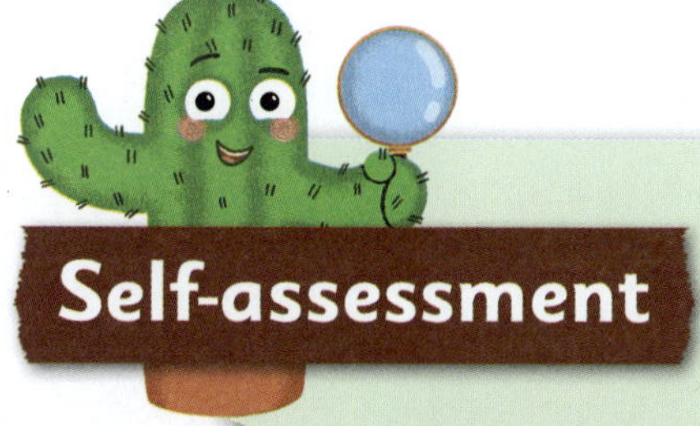

Put a circle around your best letter and word on each page.
Explain your choice to your teacher or classmate.

Have you checked your posture, pencil grip and paper position?

Have you done your warm-ups?

food

Track, trace and copy the letters and words.

f f f f f f f

f

fell fun food from far

fell

fig fox finish fish fog

fig

Trace.

above
on
below

F F F F F F

above
on
below

F

Trace and then copy the letter.

F

F

Trace and then copy this sentence on the lines below.

Freddy got quite a

Freddy

fright from the thunder.

fright

Self-assessment

Put a circle around your best letter and word on each page.
Explain your choice to your teacher or classmate.

Have you checked your posture, pencil grip and paper position?

Have you done your warm-ups?

sand

Track, trace and copy the letters and words.

s s s s s s s

s s s s s s s

s

sort sheep strong stop

sort

shock shop such sing

shock

Trace.

Trace and then copy the letter.

Trace and then copy this sentence on the lines below.

Self-assessment

Put a circle around your best letter and word on each page.
Explain your choice to your teacher or classmate.

Have you checked your posture, pencil grip and paper position?

Have you done your warm-ups?

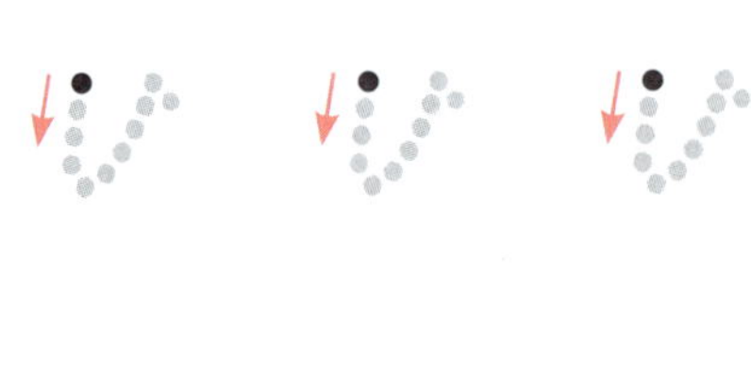

vet

Track, trace and copy the letters and words.

v v v v v v v

v v v v v v v

v

vet value venue vest

vet

van volleyball vast void

van

Trace.

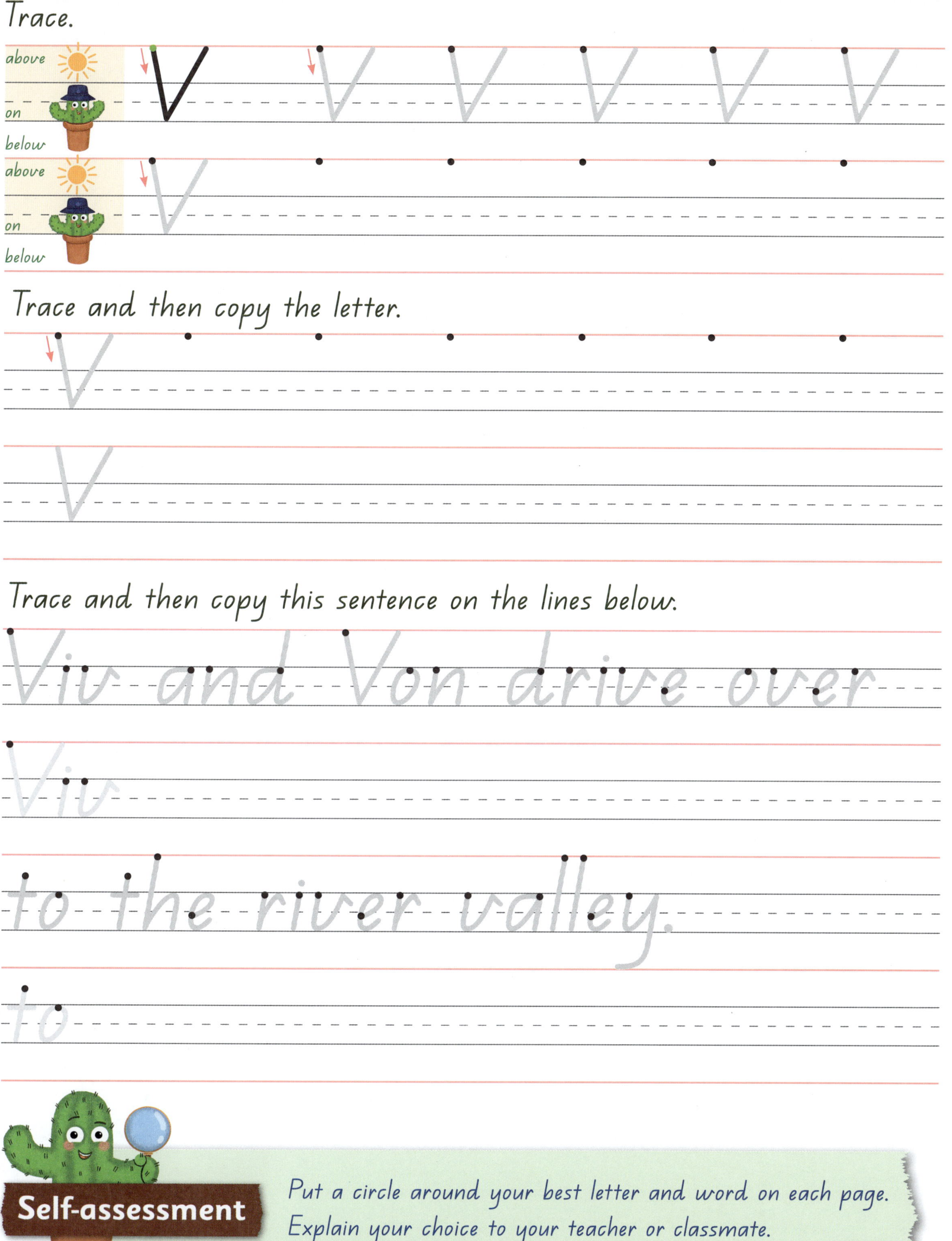

Trace and then copy the letter.

Trace and then copy this sentence on the lines below.

Self-assessment

Put a circle around your best letter and word on each page.
Explain your choice to your teacher or classmate.

Have you checked your posture, pencil grip and paper position?

Have you done your warm-ups?

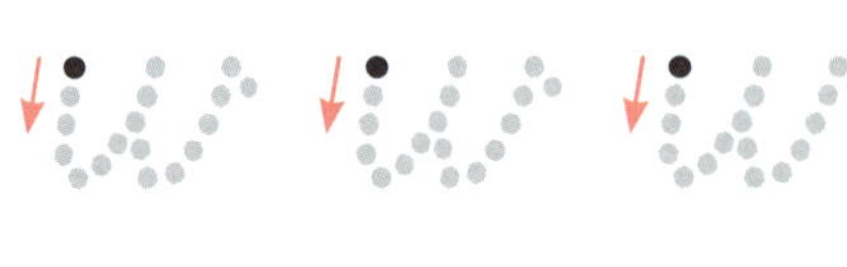

wag

Track, trace and copy the letters and words.

w w w w w w w

w w w w w w w

w

wag went way walk

wag

waiter web week weep

waiter

OXFORD UNIVERSITY PRESS

Trace.

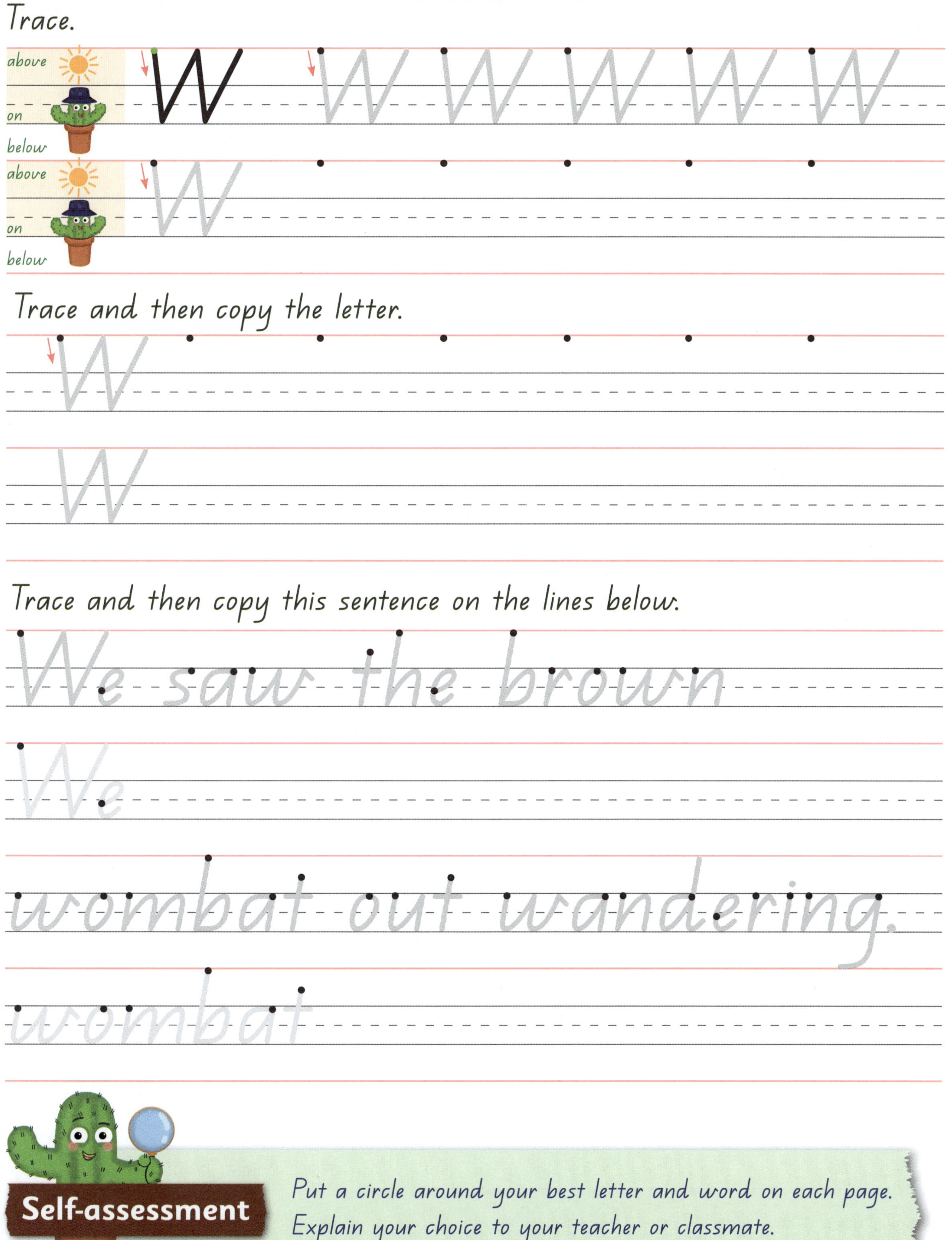

Trace and then copy the letter.

Trace and then copy this sentence on the lines below.

Self-assessment

Put a circle around your best letter and word on each page. Explain your choice to your teacher or classmate.

Have you checked your posture, pencil grip and paper position?

Have you done your warm-ups?

u u u

upset

Track, trace and copy the letters and words.

u u u u u u u

u u u u u u u

u

up us upon upset under

up

underground underneath

underground

Trace.

Trace and then copy the letter.

Trace and then copy this sentence on the lines below.

Self-assessment

Put a circle around your best letter and word on each page. Explain your choice to your teacher or classmate.

Have you checked your posture, pencil grip and paper position?

Have you done your warm-ups?

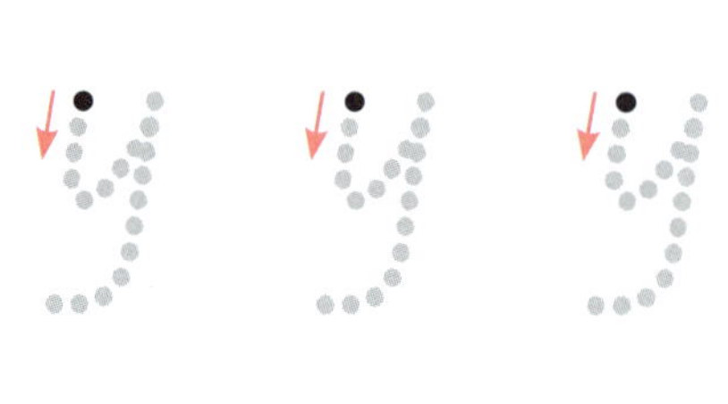

yawn

Track, trace and copy the letters and words.

y y y y y y y

y y y y y y y

y

yes yap yet yawn yak

yes

yell yum year yuck

yell

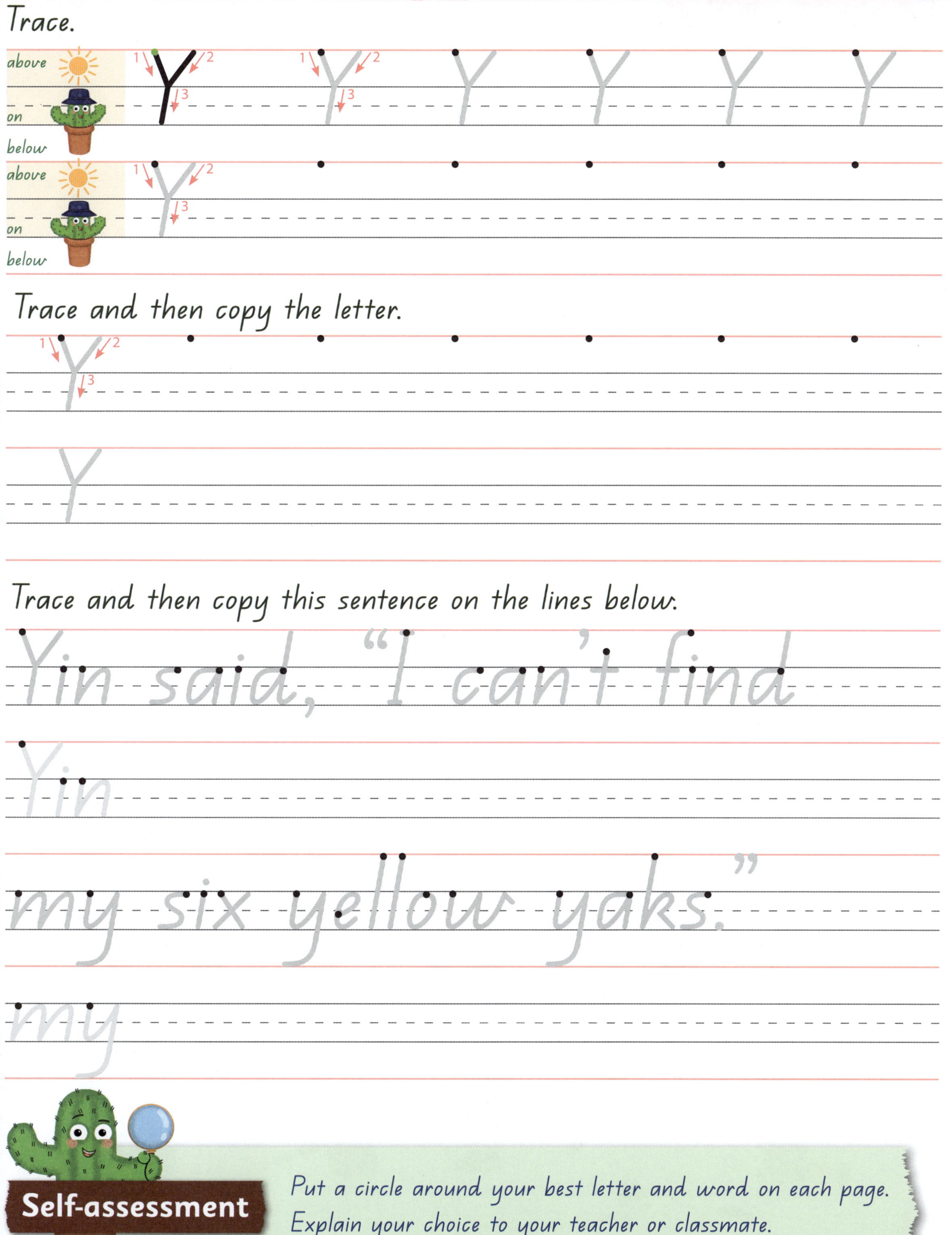

Self-assessment

Put a circle around your best letter and word on each page. Explain your choice to your teacher or classmate.

Numbers

Trace and then copy the numbers on this page and the next.

1 1

2 2

3 3

4 4

5 5

6 6

7 7

8 8

9 9

10 10

OXFORD UNIVERSITY PRESS

10 20 30 40 50

10 20 30 40 50

60 70 80 90 100

60 70 80 90 100

Trace the lower- and upper-case letters.

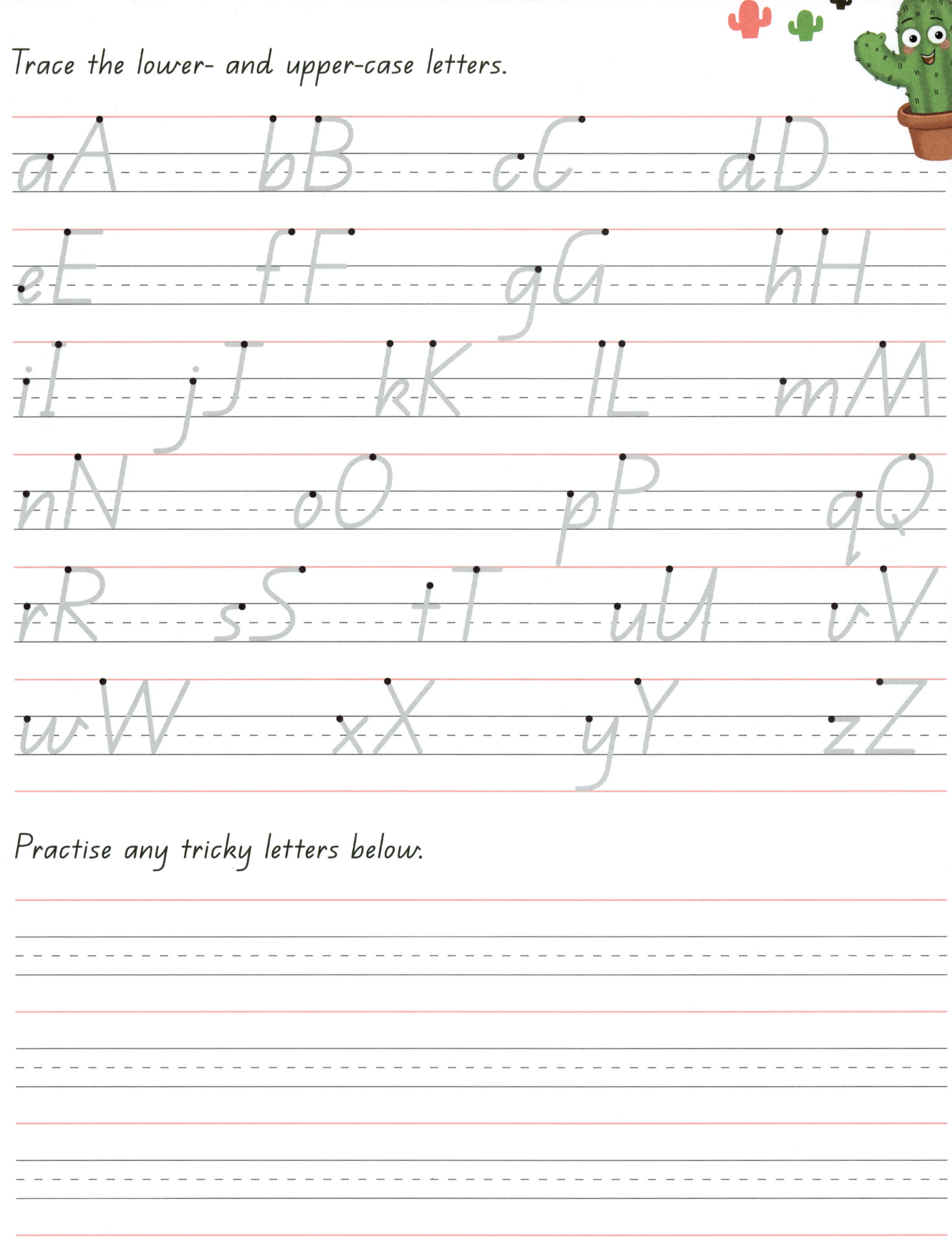

Practise any tricky letters below.

OXFORD UNIVERSITY PRESS